D1717022

BESIDE THE SEASIDE

SEASIDE JOBS

Clare Hibbert

W

FRANKLIN WATTS

LONDON • SYDNEY

First published in 2015 by
Franklin Watts
338 Euston Road
London NW1 3BH

Franklin Watts Australia
Level 17/207 Kent Street
Sydney NSW 2000

© 2015 Franklin Watts

ISBN 978 1 4451 3763 6
Library eBook ISBN 978 1 4451 3765 0

Dewey classification number: 331.1'09146

Planning and production by Discovery Books Limited
Managing editor: Paul Humphrey
Editor and picture researcher: Clare Hibbert
Design: sprout.uk.com

Printed in China

Franklin Watts is a division of Hachette Children's Books, an Hachette UK company.
www.hachette.co.uk

Photo acknowledgements: **Alamy**: 4 (Peter Noyce), 10 (Aurora Photos), 16 (Peter Titmuss), 19b (Martin Bennett), 20 (Everyday Images); **Bigstock**: 6r (fotomy), 18 (paul prescott), 22 (808wrex); **Discovery Picture Library**: 7 (Chris Fairclough), 8br (Chris Fairclough), 9b (Chris Fairclough), 14 (Chris Fairclough), 17 (Chris Fairclough), 19t (Chris Fairclough); **Shutterstock**: beachball art (Virinaflora), word box hut (AnastasiaN), seaside icons (Aleksandra Novakovic), heading strips (Inna Ogando), cover and title page (Philip Bird), 5 (Corepics VOF), 6l (spwidoff); 8t (Philip Bird), 9t (Joe Gough), 11 (Wallenrock), 12 (Monkey Business Images), 13 (wavebreakmedia), 15 (CandyBox Images); **Small Packages**: 21; **sprout.uk.com**: bucket and spade art.

Find it!
As you read this book, look out for the hidden buckets and spades. There are nine to spot.

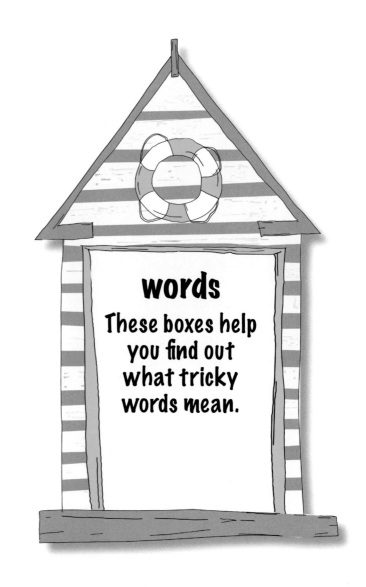

words
These boxes help you find out what tricky words mean.

CONTENTS

WORKING BY THE SEA

There are many jobs in seaside towns. Some people are teachers, doctors or police officers, just like in other towns. Others do work that can only happen by the sea, such as working in the port or harbour.

A harbour is a place where boats stay when they are not at sea. They load and unload here, too. The harbour master checks the boats coming in and out of the harbour.

Where shall we unload?

At big ports, ships bring in goods from other countries. Workers at the port (above) tell the ships' crews where to unload. A **customs** officer checks all the goods that arrive.

customs
Taxes charged on goods brought into a country.

JOBS OUT AT SEA

Some seaside towns have a fishing **fleet**. There are different kinds of fishing boats. Some are big and some are small. Some pull nets behind them through the water. Others use wire cages called traps.

We're off to catch fish!

Each fishing boat has a skipper, who is in charge of the crew. The crew run the boat. The deckhands are part of the crew. They clean up the catch of fish or shellfish.

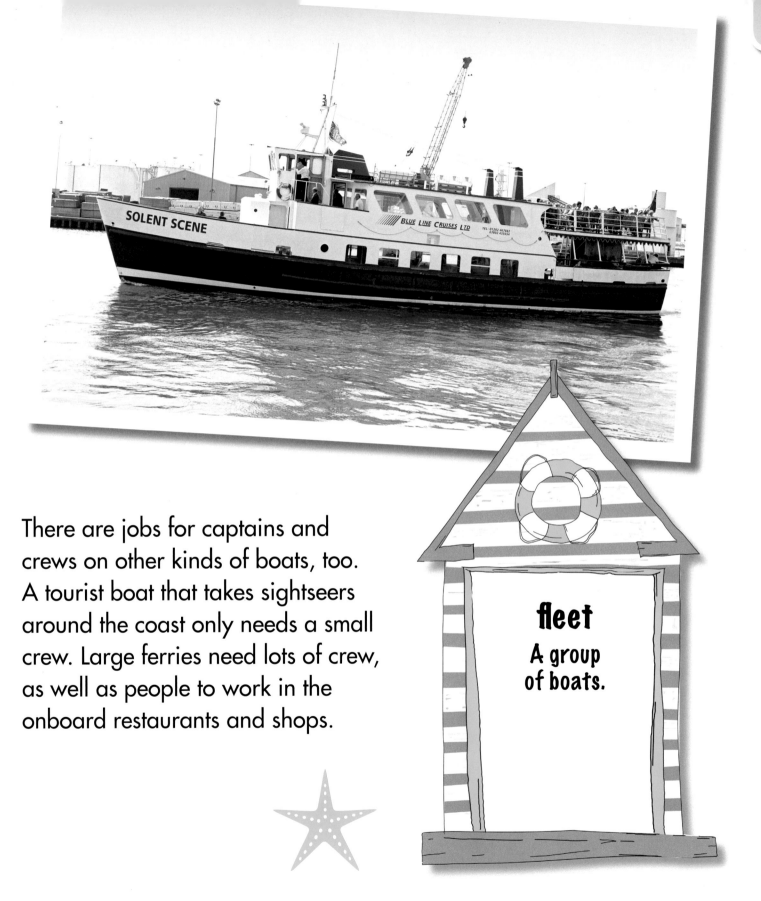

SOLENT SCENE

BLUE LINE CRUISES LTD
TEL: 01203 067082
07802 435454

There are jobs for captains and crews on other kinds of boats, too. A tourist boat that takes sightseers around the coast only needs a small crew. Large ferries need lots of crew, as well as people to work in the onboard restaurants and shops.

fleet
A group of boats.

SAFETY AT SEA

Some people in seaside towns work to keep people safe from the dangers of the sea.

It looks calm today.

Some beaches have **lifeguards**. They show people where it is safe to swim, surf or do water sports. They put up a red flag if it is too dangerous. Lifeguards rescue people in danger. They are strong swimmers.

lifeguard
Someone trained to jump in and save swimmers and surfers who get into trouble in the sea.

Coastguards help boats that get into trouble. They patrol the coast in boats or helicopters and can organise rescues. Sometimes coastguards call the lifeboat service for extra help. This organisation sends out boats and crews to rescue people in all weathers.

SPORTY JOBS

There are lots of fun sports to enjoy in seaside towns. There are sporty jobs, too. Some people sell or hire out sports equipment or wetsuits. Others work as instructors.

Some instructors teach water sports. There are plenty to choose from! Try bodyboarding, surfing (right), windsurfing or kayaking. Instructors also teach power kiting, an exciting sport for teenagers and adults that can be done on the beach or in the sea. People use the power of the wind and a kite to move along on a buggy, landboard or kite surfboard.

People also work as coaches.
They train people to do sports.
The beach is a great place to go
running, practise yoga or take part
in **bootcamp** classes.

Keep those
legs straight!

bootcamp
A keep-fit class
with very
tough exercises,
usually
outdoors.

WORK IN HOTELS

Many seaside towns have big hotels with lots of different staff working in them. The person in charge is the hotel manager. He or she works out what staff the hotel needs.

The hotel receptionists take bookings over the telephone. They sit behind a desk near the hotel entrance. They greet visitors as they arrive and give them their room keys. They take payment for the rooms.

Hotels also need people to work in the kitchen and restaurant. They prepare meals and serve them to the guests. Hotels have a team of cleaners who make the beds and keep everything clean and tidy.

staff
People who work somewhere.

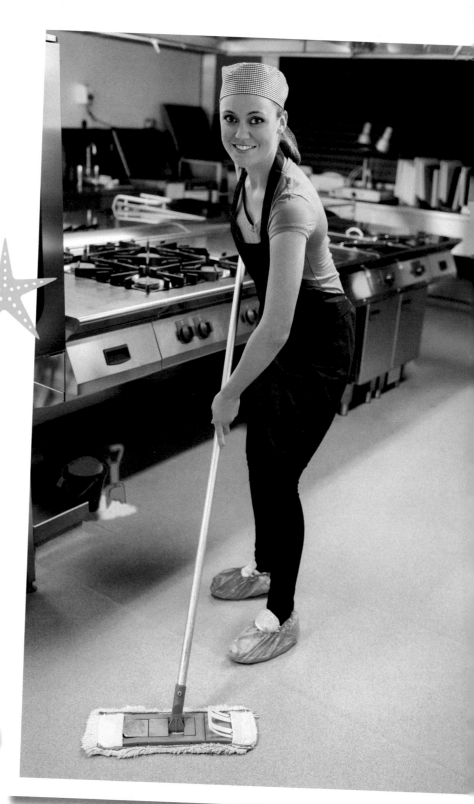

SEASIDE RESTAURANTS

There are lots of cafés and restaurants in seaside towns. These have chefs and kitchen staff who work in the kitchen preparing the food. Chefs also plan what is on the menu and order the **ingredients**.

Restaurants need waiting staff, too. They take customers' orders, make the drinks and serve the food. They also take the payment at the end of the meal and tidy up the tables.

Takeaway restaurants don't have tables for customers to eat at. They still need staff to take the orders, and hand out the food. Some takeaways have delivery staff who take the food to people's homes.

ingredients
A list of the foods which make a dish.

JOBS WITH TOURISTS

Many seaside towns are popular with tourists. Lots of the people who live in these towns have jobs looking after visitors and holidaymakers.

Some towns have a tourist information office. Its staff help holidaymakers to choose fun places to visit and exciting things to do. The staff need to know lots about the local area.

There are also jobs at all the different attractions – the places that tourists like to visit. In the funfair, people work on the rides and stalls or sell drinks and snacks. On the pier, there are jobs in the **arcades** and bars. Other people work in the town's museums or art galleries.

arcade
A place where people can play coin-operated games.

SEASIDE SELLERS

All towns have shops and markets where people work selling goods to their customers. There are some special things to sell in seaside towns.

Near the seafront, shopkeepers, stall holders and others sell fun things for the beach. The owner of this trike rides up and down the promenade, selling rubber rings, blow-up balls and other toys to customers. There are also shops that sell postcards and souvenirs, or useful items such as towels, swimwear, sunglasses and hats.

There are other jobs selling things at the seaside. Some people set up little stalls selling **whelks** and other seafood. Others work selling ice creams, drinks or snacks.

whelk
A sea snail that is good to eat.

WORKING OUTSIDE

Seaside towns take special pride in keeping their outside spaces looking good. They want holidaymakers to keep coming back!

Lots of seaside towns have gardens and parks. Gardeners and park keepers work hard to keep these looking beautiful. Teams of workers mow the grass and trim the shrubs. They clear dead leaves and keep all the flowerbeds neat. They even plant pretty flowers on the town's roundabouts.

So many lolly wrappers!

All the visitors to the town produce lots of rubbish. Most people do the right thing and put their rubbish in the bins. Refuse collectors come by in their truck to empty the bins. Some people drop their litter. The **street cleaners** have to pick this up.

street cleaner
Someone who clears rubbish off the streets.

THINGS TO DO

Now you've found out lots about seaside jobs. Are you ready for a project? Here are some ideas for fantastic follow-on activities:

1. Make a cargo collage
Look for pictures of container ships that go out to sea. They carry their cargo in large, colourful metal boxes called containers. Why not make a colourful collage of all the containers waiting on the dock to be loaded onto ships?

2. Carry out a beach job survey
In class, or with a group of friends, find out what jobs people would like to do if they lived by the seaside. Make a table that shows the results. Which job was most popular?

3. Design a menu
Fold a piece of card in half. Write the name of your restaurant on the front, and the dishes you will serve inside. Split them into starters, mains, desserts and drinks. Give everything a price.

4. Go swimming
Do you have what it takes to be a lifeguard one day? Ask an adult to take you to your nearest pool to practise your swimming. If you cannot swim yet, wear armbands and work on kicking your legs.

5. Make a water sports poster
There are so many different water sports that it's hard to remember which is which. Look in magazines for pictures of people trying out different ones and then make a fantastic poster. Look for photos of people bodyboarding, surfing, kayaking, waterskiing and power kiting.

NOTES FOR ADULTS

The **Beside the Seaside** series has been carefully planned to provide an extra resource for young children, both at school and at home. It supports and extends their learning by linking to the KS1 curriculum and beyond.

In Geography, a foundation subject at this level, the seaside is a rich and popular topic because it allows children to:

1a Ask geographical questions [for example, 'What is it like to live in this place?']

1c Express their own views about people, places and environments [for example, residents and tourists, resort attractions and places to stay]

2a Use geographical vocabulary [for example, near, far, north, south, coast, cliff]

2d Use secondary sources of information [for example, books, pictures, photographs, stories, information texts, videos, artefacts]

3a Identify and describe what places are like [for example, in terms of landscape, jobs, weather]

3c Recognise how places have become the way they are and how they are changing [for example, the importance of the fishing industry]

3d Recognise how places compare with other places [for example, compare a seaside town to a city]

4a Make observations about where things are located [for example, a bandstand on a pier or in a public park] and about other features in the environment [for example, seasonal changes in weather]

It also provides plenty of opportunities for crossover work with other subjects.

The four titles in this series split the seaside into four sub-topics:
Seaside Holidays Now and Then
Seaside Jobs
Seaside Plants and Animals
Seaside Towns

In addition to Geography, the four books support the core subjects of English, Mathematics and Science and other foundation subjects such as Art and Design, Design and Technology and History – especially if children are encouraged to get involved in the suggested extension activities on the facing page.

Reading with children

When children are learning to read, they become more confident and make quicker progress if they are exposed to as many different types of writing as possible. In particular, their reading should not only focus on fiction and stories, but on non-fiction too. The **Beside the Seaside** books offer young readers different levels of text – for example, straightforward factual sentences and fun speech bubbles. As well as maintaining children's interest, these offer children the opportunity to distinguish between different types of communication.

Make the most of your reading time. Whether it is the adult or the child who is reading, he or she should try to follow the words with his or her fingers – this is useful for non-readers, reluctant readers and confident readers alike. Pausing in your reading gives a chance for questions and to discuss the content of the pictures. For reluctant readers, try turning the reading into a game – perhaps you read alternate pages, or the child only reads speech bubble text. To further encourage interactivity with the content, there is a small artwork of a bucket and spade hidden on every main spread for children to find.

INDEX